Discovering
Unlocking your Purposeful
Life

The Mysterious Art of Ikigai

In the ancient and mysterious land of Japan, there is a practice known as Ikigai, a term that has captured the imagination of countless seekers in the quest for a fulfilling and purposeful life. At its core, Ikigai is the art of finding one's true calling, the path that leads to a life of meaning, joy, and fulfillment.

For centuries, the people of Japan have been fascinated by the concept of Ikigai. They have explored its various facets and tried to understand its mysteries, passing down the knowledge and wisdom from generation to generation. And yet, despite all their efforts, Ikigai remains elusive and enigmatic, a thing that is difficult to define, much less achieve.

So what is Ikigai? At its simplest, Ikigai is the Japanese word for "reason for being." It is the intersection of what you love, what you are good at, what the world needs, and what you can be paid for. It is the sweet spot where your passions, talents, and purpose meet, and where you can make a meaningful contribution to the world.

But Ikigai is much more than that. It is a way of life, a philosophy that guides your actions and decisions, a source of inspiration and motivation. It is the driving force that propels you forward, the light that illuminates your path, the beacon that calls you to your destiny.

To understand the mystery of Ikigai, we must look at its origins. The practice of Ikigai has its roots in the traditional

Japanese concept of Seikatsu, which refers to the pursuit of a fulfilling and rewarding life. Seikatsu is not just about achieving success or material wealth; it is about finding a sense of purpose and connection in all aspects of life, from work to relationships to hobbies.

The idea of Ikigai emerged as a natural extension of Seikatsu. It is the answer to the question of how to find your purpose in life, how to achieve a sense of fulfillment and satisfaction in all that you do. The Japanese believe that everyone has an Ikigai, a unique calling that is waiting to be discovered.

To find your Ikigai, you must first look within yourself. You must ask yourself what you are passionate about, what you are good at, what gives you a sense of purpose and meaning. You must also consider the needs of the world, what the world is lacking and what you can contribute to fill that void. And finally, you must consider the practical aspect of your Ikigai, how you can be compensated for your contribution.

But finding your Ikigai is not enough. To truly live your Ikigai, you must also cultivate a sense of balance and harmony in all aspects of your life. You must nurture your physical, emotional, and spiritual well-being, and you must cultivate a positive mindset that enables you to overcome challenges and obstacles.

The pursuit of Ikigai is a lifelong journey, a never-ending quest for self-discovery and personal growth. It is a journey that requires patience, persistence, and dedication. But the rewards are well worth the effort. When you find your Ikigai, you will experience a sense of purpose and fulfillment that is unparalleled. You will wake up every day with a sense of excitement and purpose, knowing that you are making a meaningful contribution to the world.

In conclusion, Ikigai is the mysterious art of finding your reason for being, the path that leads to a life of fulfillment, joy, and purpose. It is a journey that requires self-exploration, self-discovery, and personal growth. It is a way of life that requires balance, harmony, and a positive mindset.

The Origins of Ikigai in Japan

The ancient land of Japan is shrouded in mystery, with a rich and vibrant culture that dates back thousands of years. At the heart of this culture lies the concept of Ikigai, a term that has captured the imagination of countless seekers in the quest for a fulfilling and purposeful life. But where did this idea originate, and how has it evolved over time?

The origins of Ikigai can be traced back to the traditional Japanese concept of Seikatsu, which refers to the pursuit of a fulfilling and rewarding life. Seikatsu is based on the belief that life should be lived with a sense of purpose and connection, and that every individual has the potential to achieve a sense of fulfillment in all aspects of life.

In the early days of Japan, the concept of Seikatsu was closely tied to the Buddhist philosophy of the pursuit of enlightenment. The idea was that by living a life of purpose and connection, one could achieve a sense of inner peace and tranquility, and ultimately reach a state of enlightenment.

Over time, Seikatsu evolved into a more practical philosophy, one that was focused on achieving a sense of fulfillment in all aspects of life, from work to relationships to hobbies. This led to the emergence of the concept of Ikigai, which is essentially the answer to the question of how to find your purpose in life.

The word "Ikigai" is derived from two Japanese words: "iki," which means life, and "gai," which means value or worth. Together, these words represent the idea that everyone has a reason for being, a unique calling that is waiting to be discovered.

One of the earliest references to the concept of Ikigai can be found in the 14th century work "The Tale of the Heike," which tells the story of the Genpei War between the Taira and Minamoto clans. In the story, a warrior named Hōjō Tokiyori is said to have found his Ikigai in the practice of Zen Buddhism, which gave him a sense of purpose and direction in life.

The concept of Ikigai continued to evolve over time, with different schools of thought and traditions adding their own interpretations and perspectives. For example, in the Edo period (1603-1868), the idea of "Kokoro no Ikigai" emerged, which emphasized the importance of cultivating a sense of inner purpose and motivation.

In modern times, the concept of Ikigai has become more widely known and accepted, both in Japan and around the world. Today, there are countless books, articles, and courses that explore the topic of Ikigai, offering guidance and inspiration to those seeking a more fulfilling and purposeful life.

In conclusion, the origins of Ikigai can be traced back to the traditional Japanese concept of Seikatsu, which emphasizes the pursuit of a fulfilling and rewarding life. Over time, this concept evolved into the more practical philosophy of Ikigai, which is the art of finding one's unique calling and living a life of purpose and connection. While the idea of Ikigai has changed and evolved over time, it remains a powerful and enduring concept that has the potential to transform lives and inspire people to live their best lives.

Finding Your Purpose

As humans, we all have a deep-seated need to feel that our lives have meaning and purpose. This is why the concept of Ikigai has resonated with so many people, both in Japan and around the world. But how do we go about finding our own unique Ikigai? The search for one's purpose can be a challenging and sometimes daunting journey, but with the right tools and mindset, it is possible to unlock the key to a fulfilling and purposeful life.

The first step in the search for Ikigai is to start by asking yourself some fundamental questions. What are your passions and interests? What are your unique strengths and talents? What activities and experiences give you a sense of flow and engagement? By reflecting on these questions, you can start to gain a deeper understanding of what motivates and inspires you.

Another key factor in finding your purpose is to consider the needs and values of the world around you. What are the pressing issues and challenges that society is facing? What are the problems that you feel passionate about solving? By identifying areas where your interests and strengths intersect with the needs of the world, you can start to uncover potential avenues for your Ikigai.

It's also important to cultivate a mindset of openness and exploration. This means being willing to try new things, take risks, and embrace uncertainty. It can be tempting to stay within our comfort zones and stick with what we know, but the path to Ikigai often requires stepping outside of our familiar routines and taking on new challenges.

One powerful tool for uncovering your Ikigai is the practice of mindfulness. By cultivating a present-moment awareness and a sense of curiosity and non-judgment, you can start to observe your own thoughts and emotions with greater clarity. This can help you to identify patterns of thought and behavior that may be holding you back, and to gain a deeper understanding of your own desires and motivations.

In addition to these tools and practices, it's important to remember that the search for Ikigai is not a linear process. It's common to experience setbacks, doubts, and moments of uncertainty along the way. But by embracing the journey as a process of growth and self-discovery, rather than a destination to be reached, you can stay motivated and engaged in the search for your purpose.

Ultimately, finding your Ikigai is a deeply personal and individual journey. There is no one-size-fits-all formula for discovering your purpose in life. But by cultivating a sense of self-awareness, openness, and curiosity, you can start to uncover the unique calling that is waiting to be discovered within you. And when you do, you'll have unlocked the key to a life of fulfillment, connection, and purpose.

Embracing the Present Moment

The present moment is a powerful and transformative force in our lives. It is the place where all of our experiences and actions come together, where we can find a sense of peace and clarity, and where we can connect with the world around us in a meaningful way. But in our busy and fast-paced world, it can be all too easy to get caught up in the past or the future, and to lose touch with the power of the present moment.

One of the key principles of Ikigai is the importance of embracing the present moment. This means being fully engaged and present in our daily experiences, rather than letting our minds wander off into distractions, worries, or regrets. By learning to be present in the moment, we can cultivate a sense of mindfulness, focus, and awareness that can have profound effects on our well-being and overall sense of purpose.

One powerful tool for embracing the present moment is the practice of mindfulness meditation. By setting aside time each day to sit quietly and focus on the sensations of our breath and body, we can train our minds to be more present and attentive in our daily lives. This can help us to stay centered and grounded, even in the midst of stress and chaos.

Another key aspect of embracing the present moment is learning to let go of the past and the future. This means releasing regrets and resentments about the past, and not getting caught up in worries and anxieties about the future. By focusing on the here and now, we can create a sense of spaciousness and freedom in our minds, and open ourselves up to the full richness of the present moment.

Of course, embracing the present moment is not always easy. We are often bombarded with distractions and temptations that pull us out of the present and into our own heads. But with practice and patience, we can learn to cultivate a sense of presence and awareness that can transform our lives in powerful ways.

In the end, the practice of embracing the present moment is about learning to live fully and authentically, with a deep sense of connection and purpose in the world. By staying grounded in the here and now, we can connect with the people and experiences around us in a more meaningful way, and unlock the full potential of our Ikigai. So let us all strive to be present in the moment, to live each day with intention and purpose, and to embrace the power of the here and now.

The Role of Passion in Ikigai

Passion is a powerful force that can drive us to great heights, and it plays an important role in the philosophy of Ikigai. At its core, Ikigai is about finding a sense of purpose and meaning in our lives, and passion is one of the key ingredients that can help us achieve this goal.

Passion is a deep and intense emotion that arises when we are engaged in activities or pursuits that we find meaningful, enjoyable, and fulfilling. It is what inspires us to pursue our dreams and to pour our hearts and souls into our work, hobbies, and relationships. When we are passionate about something, we feel alive, energized, and connected to the world around us.

In the context of Ikigai, passion is an essential ingredient that can help us uncover our true purpose and potential. When we are passionate about something, we are naturally drawn to it, and we are more likely to invest the time, energy, and effort needed to develop our skills and talents in that area. This can lead to a sense of mastery and accomplishment, as well as a deep sense of satisfaction and fulfillment.

But finding our passion is not always easy. It requires us to look deep within ourselves and to be honest about our interests, values, and desires. It may involve exploring new activities, taking risks, and stepping outside of our comfort zones. It may also involve facing our fears and overcoming obstacles that stand in the way of our goals.

The key is to approach our passions with an open mind and a sense of curiosity. We should be willing to try new things, to experiment, and to explore different avenues of expression. We should also be patient and persistent, recognizing that passions can take time to develop and mature.

In the end, the role of passion in Ikigai is about finding a sense of joy, purpose, and fulfillment in our lives. It is about pursuing the things that we love and that bring us a sense of meaning and connection, and about using our passions as a vehicle for personal growth and transformation. So let us all strive to discover our passions, to cultivate them with care and attention, and to let them guide us on the path to a life of purpose and fulfillment.

Finding Meaning and Fulfillment in Your Work

Work is an essential part of our lives, and it can play a significant role in our overall sense of well-being and fulfillment. Yet for many of us, work can also be a source of stress, anxiety, and frustration. We may feel like our jobs are unfulfilling or that we are stuck in a career that doesn't align with our values or passions. However, the philosophy of Ikigai offers us a framework for finding meaning and purpose in our work, no matter what our profession may be.

At its core, Ikigai is about identifying the intersection between what we love, what we are good at, what the world needs, and what we can be paid for. When we find this intersection, we can unlock a sense of fulfillment and purpose in our work that goes beyond simply earning a paycheck.

The first step in finding meaning and fulfillment in our work is to identify our strengths and passions. This may involve reflecting on our past experiences, exploring new hobbies and interests, or seeking feedback from others. We should ask ourselves what activities bring us the most joy and energy, and what skills and talents we possess that we can bring to our work.

Once we have identified our strengths and passions, we can begin to explore how we can use them to make a positive impact in the world. This may involve finding ways to apply our skills and talents to a cause that we care deeply about, or using our work as a platform for creating positive change in our communities.

Another key aspect of finding meaning and fulfillment in our work is to cultivate a sense of purpose and connection to something greater than ourselves. This may involve identifying the core values that we hold dear and seeking out opportunities to align our work with those values. It may also involve finding ways to connect with others who share our passions and values, whether through mentorship, collaboration, or community involvement.

Of course, finding meaning and fulfillment in our work is not always easy, and it may require us to make difficult choices or take risks. We may need to be patient and persistent as we explore different opportunities and paths, and we may need to be willing to step outside of our comfort zones to find what truly resonates with us.

But in the end, the rewards of finding meaning and fulfillment in our work can be immeasurable. It can bring us a sense of purpose, fulfillment, and connection to the world around us. It can help us unlock our full potential and create a positive impact in the world. So let us all strive to find our own Ikigai in our work, and to let it guide us on the path to a life of meaning and fulfillment.

Developing a Sense of Connection and Belonging

As human beings, we all have a fundamental need for connection and belonging. We crave a sense of community and a feeling of being valued and understood by others. In fact, studies have shown that people who feel connected to others are happier, healthier, and more resilient in the face of life's challenges.

In the philosophy of Ikigai, connection and belonging are essential components of a fulfilling life. This can take many forms, whether it be a strong sense of family and community, a feeling of connection to a particular place or culture, or a shared sense of purpose and passion with others.

One way to develop a sense of connection and belonging is to seek out opportunities to connect with others who share our interests and values. This may involve joining a club, attending community events, or volunteering for a cause that we care about. By surrounding ourselves with like-minded individuals, we can feel a sense of support and belonging that can help us navigate life's challenges with greater ease.

Another important aspect of developing a sense of connection and belonging is to cultivate our relationships with our family and friends. This may involve making a conscious effort to prioritize our relationships, whether it be by setting aside regular time for quality time together, communicating openly and honestly with our loved ones, or offering support and encouragement when they need it most.

In addition to connecting with others, developing a sense of connection and belonging can also involve connecting with the world around us. This may involve finding ways to engage with nature, whether it be through hiking, gardening, or simply taking a walk in a local park. It may also involve developing an appreciation for art, culture, or history, and seeking out opportunities to explore and learn more about the world around us.

Of course, developing a sense of connection and belonging is not always easy, and it may require us to step outside of our comfort zones and take risks. We may need to be vulnerable and open to new experiences, and we may need to be patient and persistent as we seek out opportunities for connection and belonging.

But in the end, the rewards of developing a sense of connection and belonging can be immeasurable. It can bring us a sense of community, support, and understanding that can help us navigate life's challenges with greater ease. It can help us feel more fulfilled and connected to the world around us, and it can help us lead a more meaningful and purposeful life. So let us all strive to develop a strong sense of connection and belonging, and let it guide us on the path to a life of fulfillment and happiness.

The Importance of Balance in Ikigai

In the philosophy of Ikigai, balance is a fundamental concept that underpins a fulfilling and meaningful life. When we talk about balance, we refer to the idea that all aspects of our lives, from work to relationships, from health to personal development, need to be in harmony with each other in order for us to feel truly fulfilled.

One of the key principles of Ikigai is that we need to find a balance between four different elements of our lives: what we love, what we're good at, what the world needs, and what we can be paid for. This balance is known as the Ikigai balance, and it is seen as the key to unlocking our full potential and achieving a sense of purpose and fulfillment.

When we are out of balance in one or more of these areas, we may feel unfulfilled, stressed, or overwhelmed. For example, if we are working a job that we don't enjoy, we may feel like we're wasting our talents and not making a meaningful contribution to the world. On the other hand, if we are pursuing a passion that doesn't pay the bills, we may struggle to make ends meet and feel like we're not contributing to society in a meaningful way.

Finding balance in our lives requires a deep sense of self-awareness and a willingness to make changes when necessary. It may involve reevaluating our priorities and making difficult choices about how we spend our time and energy. For example, we may need to scale back on work commitments in order to spend more time with our family or pursue a personal passion. Or we may need to retrain or switch careers in order to find work that aligns more closely with our Ikigai.

But balance isn't just about finding the right mix of activities and pursuits. It's also about taking care of our physical, emotional, and spiritual well-being. This may involve developing healthy habits around exercise, nutrition, and sleep, as well as making time for self-care activities like meditation or yoga. It may also involve setting boundaries and learning to say "no" to things that drain our energy and leave us feeling stressed or overwhelmed.

Ultimately, the pursuit of balance in Ikigai is about finding a sense of peace and harmony in our lives. It's about living with intention and purpose, and making choices that align with our values and goals. By finding the right balance between work, play, and self-care, we can lead a life that is fulfilling, meaningful, and aligned with our true purpose.

Cultivating a Positive Mindset

In the philosophy of Ikigai, cultivating a positive mindset is seen as a crucial component of living a fulfilling and purposeful life. Our thoughts and beliefs shape our perceptions of the world around us and can influence our actions and decisions. When we cultivate a positive mindset, we are better able to navigate life's challenges and pursue our goals with greater confidence and resilience.

One of the key tenets of Ikigai is the idea that our thoughts and beliefs create our reality. If we believe that we are capable and worthy of achieving our goals, we are more likely to take the necessary actions to make them a reality. On the other hand, if we have negative beliefs about ourselves or our abilities, we may be more likely to hold ourselves back and miss out on opportunities.

Cultivating a positive mindset involves becoming more aware of our thoughts and learning to shift our focus towards more positive and empowering beliefs. This may involve practicing gratitude, focusing on our strengths and accomplishments, and reframing negative thoughts in a more positive light. It may also involve surrounding ourselves with positive influences, such as supportive friends and family members or uplifting media.

Another important aspect of cultivating a positive mindset is learning to embrace failure and setbacks as opportunities for growth and learning. In Ikigai, failure is seen as a necessary part of the journey towards our goals, and it is through our mistakes that we learn and grow. By reframing failure as an opportunity for growth, we can overcome our fear of failure and approach our goals with greater confidence and resilience.

In addition to these strategies, there are many other practices that can help us cultivate a positive mindset in Ikigai. These may include meditation, journaling, affirmations, and visualization exercises. By incorporating these practices into our daily routine, we can develop a more positive and empowering mindset and approach life's challenges with greater optimism and resilience.

Ultimately, cultivating a positive mindset in Ikigai is about becoming more aware of our thoughts and beliefs and learning to shift our focus towards more positive and empowering perspectives. By embracing the power of positive thinking and developing a more resilient mindset, we can overcome obstacles, achieve our goals, and live a life that is filled with purpose and meaning.

The Power of Mindfulness and Meditation

In the philosophy of Ikigai, the practice of mindfulness and meditation is seen as a powerful tool for cultivating a greater sense of presence and awareness in our daily lives. By learning to be more fully present in each moment, we can deepen our connection to ourselves, to others, and to the world around us, and cultivate a greater sense of peace, clarity, and purpose.

At its core, mindfulness is the practice of bringing our attention to the present moment, without judgment or distraction. This may involve focusing on our breath, observing our thoughts and emotions, or simply paying attention to the sights, sounds, and sensations of the world around us. Through the practice of mindfulness, we can learn to cultivate a greater sense of awareness and presence, and develop a deeper understanding of our own thoughts, emotions, and experiences.

Meditation is a powerful tool for deepening our practice of mindfulness and cultivating a greater sense of peace and inner stillness. Through the practice of meditation, we can learn to quiet our minds and connect with a deeper sense of inner wisdom and intuition. This may involve focusing on a particular object, such as a mantra or a visualization, or simply observing our thoughts and emotions as they arise and fall away.

The practice of mindfulness and meditation is particularly important in the context of Ikigai, as it can help us to develop a deeper sense of clarity and purpose in our lives. By learning to be more present in each moment, we can become more attuned to our own inner desires and motivations, and gain a greater sense of insight and intuition about what truly matters to us.

In addition to its role in cultivating greater clarity and purpose, the practice of mindfulness and meditation has also been shown to have a wide range of physical and mental health benefits. Studies have shown that regular meditation practice can reduce stress and anxiety, improve sleep quality, and enhance cognitive function and emotional regulation.

Ultimately, the power of mindfulness and meditation in Ikigai lies in its ability to connect us more deeply to ourselves, to others, and to the world around us. By learning to be more fully present in each moment, we can cultivate a greater sense of peace, clarity, and purpose, and live our lives with greater intention and fulfillment.

The Influence of Culture and Tradition on Ikigai

The philosophy of Ikigai has its roots in Japanese culture and tradition, and as such, it is deeply influenced by the values and beliefs of the Japanese people. The Japanese have a rich cultural history that dates back centuries, and many of their traditions and practices have been passed down through generations, influencing everything from their daily rituals to their approach to work and relationships.

At the heart of Japanese culture is the concept of "wa", which refers to a sense of harmony and balance in all aspects of life. This emphasis on harmony is reflected in many Japanese practices, from the traditional tea ceremony to the art of bonsai, and is an important aspect of the Ikigai philosophy.

One of the key ways that culture and tradition influence Ikigai is through the importance placed on community and social connection. In Japan, there is a strong emphasis on collective identity and group harmony, and individuals are expected to prioritize the needs of the group over their own personal desires. This emphasis on community is reflected in the Ikigai philosophy, which stresses the importance of finding meaning and fulfillment through connection and contribution to others.

Another way that culture and tradition influence Ikigai is through the emphasis on finding meaning and purpose in one's work. In Japan, there is a strong cultural expectation that individuals will find lifelong employment in a single company, and as such, work is seen as a central aspect of one's identity and purpose in life. This emphasis on work as a source of meaning and fulfillment is reflected in the Ikigai philosophy, which encourages individuals to find work that aligns with their values and passions.

The cultural emphasis on mindfulness and presence is also reflected in the Ikigai philosophy, with practices such as meditation and reflection being a central aspect of daily life in Japan. The concept of "mushin" or "mind without mind" is also important in Japanese culture, and refers to a state of complete presence and focus in the moment.

The influence of culture and tradition on Ikigai is a testament to the deep interconnection between our beliefs, values, and practices. By understanding the cultural roots of Ikigai, we can gain a greater appreciation for the philosophy and its underlying principles, and learn to apply these principles in our own lives with greater insight and wisdom. Ultimately, the philosophy of Ikigai is a testament to the power of culture and tradition in shaping our lives and helping us find purpose and meaning in the world.

Exploring Your Values and Beliefs

In order to discover your Ikigai, it is essential to take a deep look into your values and beliefs. Your values and beliefs are the foundation upon which your identity, interests, and priorities are built, and understanding them is critical to living a life of purpose and meaning.

Values can be described as the things that are most important to you in life. They are the guiding principles that help you make decisions and determine what you prioritize in your day-to-day activities. Some examples of values may include things like honesty, creativity, freedom, spirituality, or social justice. Identifying your core values can help you understand what is truly important to you, and allow you to live a life that is more aligned with your innermost desires.

Beliefs are the deeply held convictions that you have about the world around you. These beliefs can be shaped by a variety of factors, including your upbringing, culture, and personal experiences. They can be both positive and negative, and can influence your thoughts, feelings, and actions in a profound way. Understanding your beliefs is important, as they can both propel you forward and hold you back in your pursuit of Ikigai.

Exploring your values and beliefs can be a challenging and rewarding process. It may require you to confront some of your deepest fears and insecurities, and to question the assumptions that you have held for many years. However, it is a process that is well worth the effort, as it can help you gain clarity and purpose in your life.

One way to explore your values and beliefs is through self-reflection. This can be done through journaling, meditation, or simply taking time to think deeply about what matters most to you. Ask yourself questions such as, "What are the most important things in my life?", "What do I stand for?", and "What do I believe about the world and my place in it?"

Another way to explore your values and beliefs is through conversations with others. Seek out people who you admire and respect, and ask them about their own values and beliefs. This can help you gain new perspectives and insights, and allow you to see your own beliefs in a new light.

Finally, it is important to recognize that your values and beliefs may change over time. What was important to you ten years ago may not be as important to you now, and that is okay. By regularly reflecting on your values and beliefs, you can ensure that they are still aligned with who you are and who you want to become.

Ultimately, exploring your values and beliefs is a key step in discovering your Ikigai. By understanding what is most important to you and what you believe about the world, you can begin to live a life that is more purposeful, fulfilling, and true to your innermost self.

Identifying Your Strengths and Weaknesses

Knowing your strengths and weaknesses is a critical component of discovering your Ikigai. Your strengths are the things that you are naturally good at, the things that come easily to you, and the things that you enjoy doing. Your weaknesses, on the other hand, are the areas where you may struggle, or the things that you find difficult to do.

Identifying your strengths is an important step in discovering your Ikigai because it allows you to understand what you are naturally good at, and what you can bring to the world that is unique and valuable. Your strengths may include things like creativity, leadership, problem-solving, communication, or empathy. By understanding your strengths, you can identify opportunities that allow you to use these strengths, and feel a sense of purpose and fulfillment in the process.

Identifying your weaknesses is also an important step in discovering your Ikigai. While it may be difficult to confront your weaknesses, it is essential to do so in order to understand where you may need to improve, and where you may need to seek support from others. Your weaknesses may include things like time-management, organization, public speaking, or critical thinking. By understanding your weaknesses, you can work to improve in these areas, and also seek out opportunities that allow you to rely on the strengths of others.

One way to identify your strengths and weaknesses is through self-reflection. Think about the things that come naturally to you, the things that you enjoy doing, and the things that you feel proud of. These may give you clues about your strengths. Think also about the areas where you struggle, the things that you find difficult to do, and the things that make you feel insecure. These may give you clues about your weaknesses.

Another way to identify your strengths and weaknesses is to ask for feedback from others. Ask people who you trust and respect for their honest opinions about what you are good at, and what you could improve upon. This can be a valuable way to gain insights that you may not have been aware of on your own.

Finally, it is important to recognize that your strengths and weaknesses may change over time. What you were good at five years ago may not be the same as what you are good at now. By regularly reflecting on your strengths and weaknesses, you can ensure that you are always aware of your current abilities and where you may need to focus your attention in the future.

In conclusion, identifying your strengths and weaknesses is a crucial step in discovering your Ikigai. By understanding what you are naturally good at and where you may need to improve, you can make informed decisions about your career, your relationships, and your life in general. It may take some self-reflection and honesty with yourself, but the effort will be well worth it in the end.

The Role of Resilience in Ikigai

As the old saying goes, "life is a journey, not a destination." This is particularly true when it comes to the pursuit of ikigai. While finding and pursuing one's purpose is a rewarding endeavor, it is not without its challenges. Life can be unpredictable and difficult, and setbacks and disappointments are inevitable. That's why resilience is such an important factor in the pursuit of ikigai.

Resilience is the ability to bounce back from adversity, to face challenges head-on and emerge stronger on the other side. It's a trait that has been studied extensively by psychologists, who have found that resilient people tend to be more successful in all areas of life, from personal relationships to professional endeavors.

But what does resilience have to do with ikigai? Quite a lot, actually. The pursuit of one's purpose is rarely a straight line. It's a journey full of twists and turns, ups and downs, and unexpected detours. To stay on course, one needs to be resilient in the face of setbacks, obstacles, and even failures.

One way to build resilience is by cultivating a growth mindset. This is the belief that one's abilities can be developed through hard work, perseverance, and a willingness to learn from mistakes. People with a growth mindset tend to view challenges as opportunities for growth, rather than as threats to their self-worth. They also tend to be more adaptable, which is an important trait when it comes to navigating the unpredictable terrain of life.

Another key factor in resilience is social support. People who have strong connections with others, whether it's through family, friends, or a community, tend to be more resilient in the face of adversity. This is because social support provides a sense of belonging and a safety net in times of need. When we know that there are people who care about us and are there for us, we are better able to weather the storms of life.

Finally, a key aspect of resilience is self-care. This means taking care of oneself physically, emotionally, and spiritually. This can include things like getting enough sleep, eating well, exercising, practicing mindfulness, and engaging in activities that bring us joy and fulfillment. When we take care of ourselves, we are better equipped to handle the challenges that come our way.

In the pursuit of ikigai, resilience is a vital trait. It allows us to stay on course, even in the face of obstacles and setbacks. By cultivating a growth mindset, building social support, and taking care of ourselves, we can become more resilient and better equipped to pursue our purpose with confidence and determination.

Navigating Challenges and Obstacles

In the pursuit of our ikigai, we are bound to face numerous challenges and obstacles. Life has a way of testing us, and it is during these moments that our resilience is put to the test. But it is important to remember that overcoming these hurdles is what ultimately leads to growth and fulfillment.

The first step in navigating challenges and obstacles is to approach them with a positive mindset. It is easy to become discouraged when things do not go as planned, but it is important to see setbacks as opportunities for growth. This requires a shift in perspective – instead of viewing obstacles as roadblocks, we should view them as detours that may lead to unexpected discoveries.

One of the key elements of overcoming challenges is having a strong support system. We cannot go through life alone, and having people who believe in us and are there to lend a helping hand can make all the difference. This support can come from family, friends, mentors, or even online communities. It is important to build and nurture these relationships, so that when we face obstacles, we have people to turn to for guidance and encouragement.

Another important aspect of navigating challenges is to stay focused on our goals. It is easy to become sidetracked when things do not go as planned, but it is important to keep our eyes on the prize. This requires a certain degree of flexibility – we may need to adjust our plans or take a different approach, but we should never lose sight of our ultimate objective.

It is also important to remember that challenges and obstacles are not necessarily a reflection of our abilities or worth. Everyone faces setbacks at some point in their life, and it is important to view these experiences as opportunities to learn and grow. Resilience is not about being invincible, but rather about being able to bounce back from adversity.

Finally, it is important to practice self-care during times of difficulty. This means taking care of our physical, emotional, and mental health. We may need to take time off from work, seek therapy, or engage in activities that bring us joy and relaxation. When we take care of ourselves, we are better equipped to face the challenges that lie ahead.

In conclusion, navigating challenges and obstacles is an integral part of the journey towards discovering our ikigai. It requires a positive mindset, a strong support system, focus on our goals, flexibility, and self-care. When we approach obstacles with resilience and determination, we are better equipped to overcome them and ultimately achieve our full potential.

Embracing Change and Transformation

Change is inevitable, and yet it can be difficult to accept. We often find ourselves clinging to the familiar and the comfortable, even when we know that change is necessary for growth and progress. But in order to truly embrace the principles of Ikigai, we must learn to embrace change and transformation.

In Japanese culture, the concept of "mujō" captures the idea of impermanence and the transience of life. This recognition of impermanence can help us to let go of attachment to the past and embrace change in the present moment. By acknowledging the impermanence of life, we can find the courage to take risks and make changes that lead us towards our Ikigai.

One of the keys to embracing change is to approach it with an open mind and a willingness to learn. This means being willing to let go of preconceived notions and beliefs, and being open to new ideas and perspectives. When we approach change with a beginner's mind, we allow ourselves to see things in a new light and to embrace new opportunities for growth and development.

Another important aspect of embracing change is to recognize that setbacks and challenges are a natural part of the process. When we encounter obstacles or difficulties, we can use them as opportunities to learn and grow. By facing our challenges head-on and learning from our mistakes, we can become more resilient and better equipped to navigate future obstacles.

In order to embrace change, it can also be helpful to cultivate a sense of curiosity and wonder. By maintaining a sense of curiosity and wonder, we can approach change with a sense of excitement and enthusiasm, rather than fear or trepidation. This can help us to stay motivated and engaged as we pursue our Ikigai.

Of course, embracing change can also be challenging and difficult. It can be hard to let go of the familiar and the comfortable, and to step into the unknown. But by staying focused on our Ikigai and our sense of purpose, we can find the strength and courage to embrace change and transformation, and to continue growing and developing as individuals.

Ultimately, the key to embracing change and transformation is to remain grounded in our values and our sense of purpose. When we stay true to our Ikigai, we can use change as a powerful tool for growth and self-discovery, and continue on the path towards a fulfilling and meaningful life.

The Connection between Ikigai and Health

As the sun begins to set over the mountains and the day slowly draws to a close, a small group of people gather in a clearing in the forest. They come from all walks of life, young and old, rich and poor, but they are all united in their search for Ikigai, the elusive sense of purpose and meaning that is said to give life its greatest joys and satisfactions.

As they sit in a circle, a wise elder begins to speak. "My dear friends," she says, "we are here today to discuss the connection between Ikigai and health. Many people believe that being healthy is simply a matter of physical fitness, but we know that true health is much more than that. It is a state of being that encompasses our physical, mental, and emotional well-being. And it is in the pursuit of Ikigai that we can find the key to unlocking this state of being."

She goes on to explain that the pursuit of Ikigai can have a profound impact on our health in many different ways. For one thing, it can help us to develop a greater sense of purpose and meaning in life, which in turn can reduce stress and anxiety and improve our overall mental health.

"Many people today are struggling with depression, anxiety, and other mental health issues," the elder says. "And while medication and therapy can be helpful, they can only do so much. What we really need is a sense of purpose and meaning in life, something that can give us a reason to get up in the morning and face the challenges of the day. This is where Ikigai comes in. By helping us to find our purpose in life, it can give us a greater sense of meaning and fulfillment, which can go a long way in improving our mental health."

But the connection between Ikigai and health goes even deeper than that. Studies have shown that people who have a strong sense of purpose and meaning in life are less likely to develop chronic diseases such as heart disease, stroke, and diabetes. They are also more likely to recover from illness and injury more quickly and with fewer complications.

The elder goes on to explain that this is because having a strong sense of purpose and meaning in life can help to boost our immune system and improve our body's ability to fight off disease. It can also help to reduce inflammation in the body, which is a key factor in many chronic diseases.

"Ultimately," the elder says, "the pursuit of Ikigai can help us to achieve a state of wholeness and balance in our lives, which is the true definition of health. It can help us to live with greater vitality and joy, to feel connected to something greater than ourselves, and to live with a deep sense of purpose and meaning. And in doing so, it can help us to live a longer, happier, and more fulfilling life."

As the sun dips below the horizon and the group begins to disperse, the elder's words linger in the air, echoing through the forest and beyond. For those who seek Ikigai, her words are a reminder that the pursuit of purpose and meaning is not only a path to a better life, but also a path to true health and well-being.

The Benefits of Living a Purposeful Life

The journey to discovering your ikigai and living a purposeful life can be challenging, but the rewards are immeasurable. When you find and live your ikigai, you can experience numerous benefits, from improved well-being and happiness to a greater sense of meaning and fulfillment.

One of the most significant benefits of living a purposeful life is improved well-being. When you have a clear sense of purpose, you are more likely to take care of your physical, emotional, and mental health. Research has shown that people who have a sense of purpose are less likely to experience depression and anxiety and are more likely to lead healthier lifestyles, including regular exercise and a healthy diet.

Living a purposeful life can also lead to greater happiness. When you are engaged in activities that align with your values and strengths, you are more likely to experience positive emotions such as joy, contentment, and satisfaction. Moreover, having a sense of purpose can help you to develop a more optimistic outlook on life, even in the face of adversity.

Another benefit of living a purposeful life is a greater sense of meaning and fulfillment. When you know what you want to achieve in life and are actively working towards those goals, you can experience a greater sense of accomplishment and self-worth. Furthermore, living a purposeful life can give you a greater sense of connection to others, as you are more likely to engage in activities and pursuits that bring you in contact with like-minded individuals who share your values and interests.

Living a purposeful life can also provide a greater sense of direction and focus. When you have a clear sense of purpose, you know where you are going and what you want to achieve. This can help you to make more deliberate choices in your life, from the career you pursue to the people you choose to spend time with. Moreover, having a sense of purpose can help you to overcome obstacles and challenges, as you have a clear motivation to persist in the face of adversity.

Finally, living a purposeful life can help you to leave a positive impact on the world around you. When you are engaged in activities that align with your values and goals, you can make a meaningful contribution to society, whether through your work, your volunteering, or your personal relationships. This can provide a sense of meaning and purpose that goes beyond the individual level, contributing to a greater sense of social cohesion and community.

In conclusion, living a purposeful life can lead to numerous benefits, from improved well-being and happiness to a greater sense of meaning and fulfillment. While the journey to finding your ikigai may be challenging, the rewards are immeasurable. By identifying and pursuing your purpose, you can live a more fulfilling and satisfying life, both for yourself and for those around you.

The Intersection of Ikigai and Creativity

In the world of Ikigai, creativity is not just a means of artistic expression, but a vital component of a purposeful life. Creativity is defined as the ability to come up with new and innovative ideas, solutions, and approaches to life's challenges. When we engage in creative pursuits, we tap into a deep well of inspiration and self-expression that helps us unlock our fullest potential.

Creativity is not limited to the arts, but can be applied to any aspect of life, from problem-solving and critical thinking to building and designing. When we embrace our creative side, we allow ourselves to think outside the box, to explore new possibilities, and to push the boundaries of what we thought was possible.

The connection between Ikigai and creativity is rooted in the concept of self-discovery. By exploring our interests and passions, we gain a deeper understanding of who we are and what brings us joy. When we identify our Ikigai, we can then use our creative talents to bring that purpose to life in unique and meaningful ways.

For example, someone who has discovered their Ikigai in teaching may use their creativity to design engaging lesson plans and find new ways to connect with their students. A musician who has found their Ikigai in performing may use their creativity to compose and record new music that resonates with their audience.

Creativity is not just about producing something new, but also about finding new ways to approach old problems. By looking at challenges with a creative mindset, we can come up with innovative solutions and push past our limitations.

At the same time, engaging in creative pursuits can also provide a sense of fulfillment and satisfaction. Whether it's through writing, painting, cooking, or any other creative outlet, we can find a sense of joy and accomplishment in the process of bringing our ideas to life.

However, the intersection of Ikigai and creativity is not always a straightforward one. It can be challenging to find the time, resources, and inspiration to pursue creative endeavors, especially in a world that often prioritizes productivity over self-expression. Additionally, fear of failure or self-doubt can hold us back from exploring our creative side.

To overcome these challenges, it's important to approach creativity with an open mind and a willingness to experiment. It's also important to make time for creative pursuits, even if it's just a few minutes a day, and to seek out opportunities to collaborate with others and learn from their perspectives.

Ultimately, the intersection of Ikigai and creativity is a powerful one, offering us a unique and fulfilling way to bring our purpose to life. By embracing our creative side and finding new ways to express ourselves, we can unlock our fullest potential and live a life filled with meaning, purpose, and joy.

The Importance of Self-Care in Ikigai

Living a life with purpose can be a fulfilling and rewarding experience, but it can also be exhausting and demanding. Pursuing your passions and working towards your goals can require a great deal of time, effort, and energy. That's why it's essential to practice self-care as a part of your ikigai journey.

Self-care refers to the intentional actions we take to nurture our physical, emotional, and mental well-being. It involves prioritizing our needs and making choices that support our health and happiness. Self-care is not selfish; it's a vital aspect of maintaining a healthy and balanced life.

One of the keys to practicing self-care is developing self-awareness. By understanding our needs, values, and limitations, we can make choices that align with our goals and values. When we neglect our needs, we risk burning out, becoming overwhelmed, and losing sight of our purpose.

Physical self-care includes taking care of your body, such as eating a healthy diet, getting enough sleep, and engaging in regular exercise. Taking care of your physical health not only makes you feel better but also boosts your mood and energy levels.

Emotional self-care involves tending to your emotions and feelings. This could involve spending time with loved ones, engaging in creative activities, or practicing relaxation techniques such as meditation or yoga. Emotional self-care allows you to process your emotions and maintain healthy relationships with those around you.

Mental self-care involves taking care of your mind. This could involve engaging in activities that challenge you, such as learning a new skill, practicing a hobby you enjoy, or engaging in deep conversations with others. Mental self-care helps keep your mind sharp and focused.

Spiritual self-care involves nourishing your soul or connecting with a higher power. This could involve attending religious services, practicing mindfulness, or spending time in nature. Spiritual self-care can help you connect with a deeper sense of purpose and meaning.

Incorporating self-care practices into your daily routine can help you maintain balance and perspective in your life. It's important to remember that self-care is not a one-time event but an ongoing process. Making self-care a habit can help you stay on track with your goals and live a more fulfilling and purposeful life.

In conclusion, self-care is a vital aspect of practicing ikigai. It allows us to maintain balance, stay healthy, and pursue our passions without burning out. By practicing self-care, we can stay connected to our purpose and lead fulfilling lives.

Developing a Growth Mindset

As humans, we are constantly evolving and growing, both intellectually and emotionally. We are always learning new things, whether consciously or subconsciously. Developing a growth mindset is essential to leading a fulfilling life and pursuing your ikigai.

A growth mindset is the belief that your abilities and intelligence can be developed through dedication, hard work, and a willingness to learn from your mistakes. This mindset is based on the idea that your potential is not fixed and can be improved through effort and perseverance.

In contrast, a fixed mindset is the belief that your abilities and intelligence are set in stone and cannot be changed. People with a fixed mindset tend to avoid challenges and give up easily, believing that their talents and abilities are predetermined.

Developing a growth mindset can help you overcome obstacles, pursue your passions, and achieve your goals. Here are some ways to cultivate a growth mindset:

1. Embrace challenges: Instead of avoiding difficult tasks, see them as opportunities for growth and learning. Embrace the process of learning and the potential for growth, even if it means making mistakes and experiencing failure.
2. Focus on effort and progress: Instead of fixating on results, focus on the effort and progress you make along the way. Celebrate the small victories and use them as motivation to keep going.

3. Learn from mistakes: Instead of being discouraged by mistakes, see them as opportunities to learn and improve. Reflect on what went wrong, how you can do better next time, and what you learned from the experience.
4. Seek out feedback: Instead of shying away from criticism, seek out constructive feedback from others. Use it as an opportunity to learn and grow, and use the feedback to improve your performance.
5. Believe in your ability to change: Instead of believing that your abilities and intelligence are fixed, believe that you can improve and grow through effort and perseverance. Trust in your ability to learn and adapt, and have faith in your potential to achieve your goals.

Developing a growth mindset takes time and effort, but the benefits are immense. With a growth mindset, you can overcome obstacles, pursue your passions, and achieve your goals, all while cultivating a sense of purpose and fulfillment in your life.

The Role of Gratitude in Ikigai

Mitsuko closed her eyes and took a deep breath. As she exhaled, she whispered, "Arigatou." She repeated this word three times, each time feeling the gratitude fill her heart.

Gratitude was an important aspect of Mitsuko's daily practice of Ikigai. She knew that expressing gratitude was not only polite in Japanese culture, but it was also a key element in living a fulfilling and purposeful life. Mitsuko had learned from her grandmother that expressing gratitude was an essential part of a healthy and happy life.

In this chapter, we will explore the role of gratitude in Ikigai and how expressing gratitude can have a significant impact on our lives.

Gratitude is defined as the quality of being thankful and showing appreciation for something or someone. It is a fundamental human emotion that can be expressed in many ways, such as through words, actions, or thoughts. Gratitude can be directed towards specific people, events, or even the mundane things we often take for granted.

In Ikigai, gratitude is considered a foundational practice. Expressing gratitude can help us to appreciate the things we have in our lives and cultivate a positive mindset. Gratitude helps us to focus on what is good in our lives, rather than dwelling on the negative. When we express gratitude, we open ourselves up to receiving more positive experiences, creating a cycle of positivity and abundance.

When we are grateful, we become more aware of the interconnectedness of all things. We begin to see how our actions and choices impact those around us, and how we are all part of a larger community. Expressing gratitude can help us to cultivate a sense of empathy and compassion for others, as we begin to see the world through their eyes.

Gratitude can also help us to cope with difficult situations. When we experience challenges, it can be easy to focus on what we lack or what we wish we had. However, when we express gratitude for what we do have, we can shift our focus to what is possible, rather than what is not. Gratitude can help us to reframe our perspective and find solutions to problems.

Mitsuko had learned that expressing gratitude was not just about saying "thank you." It was about cultivating a mindset of appreciation and finding joy in the little things. For example, she would express gratitude for the sun shining or the birds singing, for the food on her plate or the smile from a stranger.

To incorporate gratitude into your Ikigai practice, start by taking a few moments each day to reflect on what you are grateful for. Write down three things you appreciate in your life, no matter how small they may seem. You can also express gratitude directly to someone who has made a positive impact in your life, or even to yourself for something you have accomplished.

Remember, gratitude is not just about saying "thank you." It is about cultivating a sense of appreciation and joy for the things we have in our lives. By incorporating gratitude into our Ikigai practice, we can find greater fulfillment and purpose in our daily lives.

Discovering Your Ikigai Community

The search for ikigai is a deeply personal journey, but it is not one that has to be taken alone. In fact, the support and encouragement of like-minded individuals can be an essential part of the process. This is where finding your ikigai community comes in.

At its core, an ikigai community is a group of people who share similar values, interests, and goals related to their purpose and passion in life. Such a community can provide a sense of belonging and validation, which in turn can be a source of motivation and inspiration. It can also offer practical support in the form of resources, networking, and accountability.

Finding your ikigai community may require some effort and experimentation, but it can be a rewarding and fulfilling process. Here are some steps you can take to discover your tribe:

1. Identify your interests and passions.

To find your ikigai community, you need to first identify what matters to you. What are your interests, hobbies, and passions? What activities or causes light you up? This could be anything from writing to yoga, from social justice to environmental activism. Once you have a clear sense of what you care about, you can begin to look for groups that share your interests.

2. Research and explore.

The internet is a great place to start your search for an ikigai community. Look for online forums, Facebook groups, and other social media platforms where people discuss topics related to your interests. You can also search for local meetups or events related to your hobbies and passions.

If you're not sure where to begin, start with a general search for "ikigai communities" or "purpose-driven groups" and see what comes up. You may find some organizations or communities that resonate with you.

3. Attend events and meetings.

Once you've identified some potential communities, attend their events or meetings to get a feel for the group. This could be a yoga class, a writing workshop, a volunteer project, or a book club meeting. Pay attention to the vibe of the group and how you feel while you're there. Do you feel welcomed and comfortable? Do you share the same values and goals as the other members? This can give you a good indication of whether or not the group is a good fit for you.

4. Connect with others.

If you find a group that feels like a good match, start connecting with the other members. Introduce yourself, share your interests and goals, and listen to what others have to say. Building relationships with others who share your passion can be a powerful source of support and motivation.

5. Share your own story.

As you get to know your ikigai community, don't be afraid to share your own story and struggles. Being vulnerable and authentic can help you build deeper connections and may even inspire others. Your journey towards discovering your ikigai can be a source of inspiration for others.

6. Pay it forward.

As you gain support and inspiration from your ikigai community, consider how you can pay it forward. Share your own insights and experiences, offer support and encouragement to others, and contribute to the group in any way you can. This will help to strengthen the community and create a virtuous cycle of support and growth.

In the end, finding your ikigai community is about finding your tribe, a group of people who will support and encourage you in your journey towards living a purposeful and fulfilling life. With some effort and a little bit of serendipity, you can find your tribe and unlock the full potential of your ikigai.

Nurturing Relationships and Connections

As humans, we are social beings who crave connection and companionship. In the pursuit of ikigai, building and nurturing relationships is crucial. Whether it's a partner, family member, friend, or colleague, healthy and meaningful relationships can bring joy, support, and motivation to achieve our goals.

Building relationships can be a challenge, and it requires effort and time to foster meaningful connections. But with the right mindset and attitude, it is possible to build relationships that are fulfilling and contribute to our overall sense of purpose and well-being.

One way to build and nurture relationships is through effective communication. Communication involves not just speaking, but also listening and understanding. It is important to be an active listener, to pay attention to what the other person is saying, and to ask questions to clarify any confusion. In doing so, we can deepen our understanding of the other person's perspectives and experiences, which can strengthen our relationship.

Another important aspect of nurturing relationships is maintaining boundaries. This involves respecting the other person's needs and priorities while still being clear about our own. Boundaries can be both physical and emotional, and setting them can help avoid misunderstandings and conflicts in relationships.

In addition to effective communication and maintaining boundaries, showing appreciation and kindness towards others can also help foster meaningful relationships. Expressing gratitude and acknowledging the efforts and contributions of others can go a long way in building trust and respect.

But building and nurturing relationships is not just about giving. It's also important to receive support and care from others. Accepting help and acknowledging our vulnerabilities can help us build deeper connections with those around us.

Ultimately, building and nurturing relationships is about finding a balance between giving and receiving, understanding and respecting boundaries, and communicating effectively. By doing so, we can create a community of individuals who support and inspire each other in the pursuit of our individual and collective ikigai.

Embracing the Journey of Self-Discovery

As I sat at my desk, gazing out at the world beyond, I couldn't help but think of the journey that lay ahead. The journey of self-discovery. The journey towards finding one's ikigai.

For many of us, the journey of self-discovery can be a daunting one. It requires us to be vulnerable, to look deep within ourselves, and to confront our fears and insecurities. But it is a journey that is worth taking. A journey that can lead to a life of purpose, fulfillment, and joy.

The first step on this journey is to acknowledge that we are all unique. Each of us has our own set of experiences, beliefs, and values that have shaped who we are today. And it is only by understanding and embracing these unique aspects of ourselves that we can truly discover our ikigai.

The journey of self-discovery is not a linear one. It is full of twists and turns, ups and downs, and moments of uncertainty. But through it all, we must remember to be kind to ourselves. To treat ourselves with the same kindness and compassion that we would extend to a dear friend.

As we embark on this journey, we must also be willing to let go of the things that no longer serve us. To let go of the fears, doubts, and insecurities that hold us back from reaching our full potential. It is only by letting go of these things that we can create space for new experiences, new perspectives, and new opportunities to come into our lives.

And as we journey deeper into the unknown, we must also be willing to embrace the discomfort that comes with self-discovery. To push through the discomfort, to confront our fears head-on, and to keep moving forward even when the road ahead seems dark and uncertain.

But most importantly, we must remember that the journey of self-discovery is not a solo one. We all need a support system. A community of like-minded individuals who can offer us guidance, support, and encouragement along the way. A community that can help us discover our ikigai and live a life of purpose and meaning.

So let us embrace this journey of self-discovery with open hearts and minds. Let us be patient with ourselves as we explore the depths of our being. And let us remember that the journey is just as important as the destination. For it is in the journey that we discover who we truly are and what we are meant to do in this world.

Overcoming Fear and Limiting Beliefs

In life, we often encounter fear and limiting beliefs that hold us back from achieving our goals and reaching our full potential. These fears can range from the fear of failure to the fear of the unknown. It is essential to recognize these fears and learn how to overcome them if we want to live a purposeful and fulfilling life.

To overcome fear and limiting beliefs, we must first identify them. We must recognize the negative self-talk that arises within us and challenge it. We must question the validity of these beliefs and ask ourselves whether they are based on reality or simply our imagination. Often, our fears are not grounded in reality but are the result of our minds playing tricks on us.

Once we identify our fears and limiting beliefs, we can begin to take steps to overcome them. One way to do this is to break them down into smaller, more manageable steps. By doing this, we can build confidence and gradually push ourselves outside of our comfort zones.

Another way to overcome fear and limiting beliefs is to seek the support of others. It can be helpful to talk to people who have overcome similar challenges or seek out a mentor who can guide us through the process. By building a support system, we can gain perspective and reassurance as we work through our fears.

It is important to remember that overcoming fear and limiting beliefs is not a one-time event but an ongoing process. It requires a willingness to take risks, try new things, and be open to the unknown. By embracing a growth mindset and focusing on learning and growth, we can continually push ourselves to be our best selves.

In the end, overcoming fear and limiting beliefs is essential to finding our Ikigai. It is only when we can push past our fears that we can truly discover our purpose and live a fulfilling life. So, embrace the journey of self-discovery, face your fears, and don't let limiting beliefs hold you back from reaching your full potential.

Creating a Plan for Living Your Ikigai

As one embarks on the journey to find their Ikigai, they may begin to feel overwhelmed by the many factors that influence this search. The journey requires introspection, self-reflection, and an open mind, but it also requires practical steps to turn the discoveries and insights gained along the way into actionable plans. Without a concrete plan, the many revelations that come along with the search for Ikigai may quickly become muddled and lost in the busyness of daily life.

Creating a plan for living your Ikigai is about taking the time to set intentions and create actionable steps that will bring you closer to living a purposeful life. This process begins by acknowledging that change takes time and that the journey to finding and living your Ikigai is not a straight line. It's a process that requires patience, flexibility, and a willingness to adapt.

The first step in creating a plan for living your Ikigai is to take stock of what you have learned about yourself and your values during the search for your purpose. Reflect on your strengths and weaknesses, your passions, your beliefs, and the things that bring you joy. Consider how you can use these insights to build a life that aligns with your values and provides a sense of fulfillment.

The next step is to set achievable goals. Goals that are specific, measurable, and achievable are more likely to be accomplished. By setting goals, you can break down the journey to living your Ikigai into small, manageable steps. Perhaps your goal is to start a new hobby that aligns with your passions or to connect with like-minded individuals who share your interests. Or maybe you want to explore a new career path that is more aligned with your purpose. Whatever your goals may be, it's important to make them realistic and achievable.

Once you have established your goals, it's essential to create a plan for achieving them. This plan should include specific steps that will help you reach your goals, along with timelines and deadlines for each step. Consider what resources you may need to achieve your goals, such as time, money, or support from friends or family. Make sure that your plan is flexible, and be willing to adapt as necessary. Remember, the journey to finding your Ikigai is not a straight line, and it's essential to be patient and adaptable as you work toward your goals.

To ensure that you stay on track, it's important to track your progress. Celebrate your achievements and make note of any setbacks or challenges that you encounter along the way. By tracking your progress, you can identify patterns and adjust your plan accordingly.

In conclusion, creating a plan for living your Ikigai is a critical step in the journey toward living a purposeful life. It's about taking the insights and revelations that you have gained along the way and turning them into actionable steps that align with your values and bring you fulfillment. Remember to be patient, adaptable, and flexible as you work toward your goals. With a solid plan in place, you can confidently move forward on your journey to living your Ikigai.

Celebrating Your Ikigai

The concept of Ikigai is not only a philosophy, but also a way of life. The journey to discovering and living one's Ikigai is not always an easy one, but it is a journey that is filled with self-discovery, growth, and fulfillment.

When one finally discovers their Ikigai, it is a time for celebration. It means that they have found their purpose in life, and they are now living a fulfilling and meaningful existence. It is a time to reflect on the hard work and dedication that was required to get there, and to feel proud of what has been accomplished.

For some, living their Ikigai may involve a career change or a major life shift. For others, it may mean simply incorporating new practices into their daily routine or prioritizing different aspects of their life. Whatever the case may be, it is important to take time to acknowledge and celebrate the achievement.

Celebrating one's Ikigai can take many different forms. It could be as simple as taking a moment to acknowledge the progress that has been made, or it could be as grand as throwing a party with friends and loved ones. The important thing is to take time to reflect on the journey and to recognize the growth that has been achieved.

It is also important to remember that discovering and living one's Ikigai is not a one-time event. It is a continuous journey that requires ongoing attention and dedication. It is important to continually reflect on one's values, beliefs, and passions, and to make adjustments as needed.

Living one's Ikigai is not only beneficial for the individual, but also for those around them. When one is living a fulfilling and purposeful life, they are able to positively impact the world around them. By living their own truth, they can inspire others to do the same, and create a ripple effect that spreads positivity and fulfillment throughout the world.

In conclusion, celebrating one's Ikigai is an important part of the journey towards living a fulfilling life. It is a time to reflect on the hard work and dedication that has been put in, and to acknowledge the progress that has been made. It is also a time to remember that living one's Ikigai is an ongoing journey, and to continually reflect on one's values, beliefs, and passions. By living one's truth, individuals can positively impact the world around them, and inspire others to do the same.

The Legacy of Ikigai: Living a Life of Purpose

As we come to the end of this journey towards discovering our ikigai, it is important to reflect on the legacy that we hope to leave behind. When we are living a life of purpose, we are not just fulfilling our own potential, but we are also contributing to the world in a positive way. Our unique skills, passions, and values can be used to create positive change in our communities, our countries, and even the world.

Think about the people in history who have left a lasting legacy. They all had one thing in common: they had a strong sense of purpose and were driven by a desire to make a positive impact on the world. Whether it was through their art, their science, their political activism, or their social work, they left an indelible mark on the world.

The legacy that we leave behind is not just about what we accomplish, but how we live our lives. When we live a life of purpose, we inspire others to do the same. We create a ripple effect that spreads far beyond ourselves, and we make the world a better place for future generations.

Living a life of purpose is not always easy. It requires courage, persistence, and a willingness to take risks. We must be willing to step outside our comfort zones and embrace the unknown. We must be willing to fail, to make mistakes, and to learn from them. But in doing so, we discover our true potential and unlock a world of possibilities.

As we reflect on the legacy that we hope to leave behind, it is important to remember that it is never too late to start living a life of purpose. It is never too late to discover our ikigai and begin to use our unique gifts and talents to make a positive impact on the world. It is never too late to start a new chapter in our lives, to take a new path, and to embrace the journey of self-discovery.

In the end, the legacy of ikigai is about living a life of meaning and purpose, and leaving the world a better place than we found it. It is about inspiring others to do the same and creating a ripple effect that will continue long after we are gone. So let us embrace our ikigai, celebrate our unique strengths and talents, and use them to make a positive impact on the world. Let us create a legacy that we can be proud of, and that will inspire future generations to do the same.

Conclusion

I want to take a moment to reflect on what we have learned about Ikigai and how it can shape our lives for the better.

Ikigai is a concept that has been around for centuries, rooted in the rich cultural traditions of Japan. However, its universal principles can be applied to anyone, anywhere in the world. It's about finding your unique sense of purpose and meaning in life, and then actively pursuing it.

Throughout this book, we've explored the different components of Ikigai, including identifying our values and strengths, developing a growth mindset, nurturing relationships, and practicing self-care, among others. We've also looked at the challenges and obstacles that can arise when pursuing our Ikigai and the importance of resilience, mindfulness, and a positive mindset in overcoming them.

We've seen how our culture and traditions can influence our Ikigai and how the pursuit of purpose and fulfillment can have a profound impact on our health, creativity, and overall well-being. We've also examined how living a life of purpose can help us overcome fear and limiting beliefs, create a plan for achieving our goals, and ultimately leave a positive legacy.

But beyond all of this, what I hope you take away from this book is the idea that each of us has the power to create a life that is fulfilling and purposeful. It doesn't matter where you come from or what your background is. It's about taking the time to reflect on what truly matters to you and then taking action to make it a reality.

The journey towards Ikigai is not always an easy one, and it requires effort, patience, and perseverance. However, the rewards of living a life of purpose and meaning are immeasurable. It's about celebrating the small wins, learning from the setbacks, and staying true to your values and beliefs.

So as you continue on your journey towards living a fulfilling life, remember that your Ikigai is not something that can be found overnight. It's a process of self-discovery and growth that will continue to evolve throughout your life. But by embracing this process and remaining committed to your purpose, you have the power to create a life that is truly extraordinary.

Thank you for taking the time to explore the world of Ikigai with me. May you find joy and purpose in all that you do.

Dear reader,

Thank you for taking the time to read this work. It was an honor to have you journey with us through the concepts and practices of ikigai.

I hope that the ideas and stories shared in these pages have inspired you to live a more purposeful and fulfilling life. Remember that living your ikigai is a continuous process of self-discovery, growth, and celebration.

If you found this work valuable, please consider leaving a positive review. Your feedback will not only help us to improve but also inspire others to embark on their journey towards a more meaningful and joyful life.

Once again, thank you for your time and support. May you continue to discover and live your ikigai.

Sincerely,

Kars Kato

Printed in Great Britain
by Amazon